*Even without doing any activity you can still manifest wh
if you organize these four dimensions in one direction and keep it unv
for a certain period of time.*

"Now he believes Shiva will do it for him and it will happen."

So is *Shiva* going to come and build your house?

'No, i want you to understand, God will not lift his little finger for you.'

What has not happened until now on this planet can happen tomorrow, human beings are capable
of making it happen tomorrow.

*Everything we as human beings have created on this planet was essentially first created in our
minds.*

All that you see which is human work on this planet, *first found expression in the mind.*
Then it got *manifested* in the outside world.

The *wonderful* things that we have done on this planet, and the *horrible* things that we have done
on this planet, both have come from the *human mind.*

So if you are concerned as to what we create in this world,
it is extremely important that,
first of all,
we learn to *create* the right things in our mind.

How we keep our minds.

If we do not have the power to keep our minds the way we want it,
what we create in the world is also going to be very accidental and haphazard.

So learning to *create our minds* the way we *want* is the *basis* of
creating the world the way we *want.*

There is a wonderful story in the yogic lore;

On a certain day, a man went for a walk,
he went for a long walk.
Accidentally,
unaware,
he walked into paradise.

Fortunate, isn't he?

He just took a walk and ended up in paradise.

After this long walk,
he felt a little tired.

So he thought,
'oh i am tired,
i wish i could rest somewhere.'

He looked around,
over there was a nice tree, under which there was very cushiny grass.

So it was inviting,
he went and put his head down there and slept.

After a few hours he woke up.

Well rested.

And he thought,
'i am well rested, but i am feeling hungry, i wish i had something to eat.'

And he thought about all the nice things that he ever wanted to eat in his life.
And instantly, all those things appeared in front of him.
You need to understand there the service is like that.
Hungry people don't ask questions, food came and he ate.
Stomach became full.

Then he thought,
'my stomach is full, i wish i had something to drink.'

All the nice things that he wanted to drink, he thought about it, and all of them just appeared,
in front of him.
Drinking people also don't ask questions.
So he drank.

Now, with a little bit of alcohol in him,
you know *Charles Darwin told you all of you are monkeys that your tail fell away,*
not me,
Charles Darwin told you, that you were all monkeys and your tail fell away,
and then you became human.
Yes, definitely the tail fell away.
But the monkey;

In *yoga,*
we always refer to an unestablished mind as *'markata',*
which means a *monkey.*

Why we are referring to the mind as a monkey is,
What are the qualities of a monkey?
One thing about a monkey is its unnecessary movement.
And another thing about the monkey is,
if i say you're monkeying somebody,
what does it mean,
imitation.

Monkey and imitation have become synonymous.
So these two essential qualities, of a monkey,
are very much the qualities of an unestablished mind.

Unnecessary movement,
you don't have to learn it from the monkey-you can teach it to the monkey,
and *imitation* is full time job of the mind.

So when these two qualities are on a mind is referred to as a monkey.

So this monkey became active within him.

He just looked around and thought,
'What the hell is happening here,
i asked for food, food came,
i asked for drink, drink came.
There must be ghosts around here.'

And ghosts came.

'Oh the ghosts have come, they're going to surround me and torture me,'
he thought.

Immediately the ghosts surrounded him and started torturing him.

Then he started screaming in pain,
'oh they're going to kill me.'

And he died.

Just now he said he is a fortunate being.

The problem was he was sitting under a *Kalpavriksha,*
or a wishing tree.
He asked for food, food came.
He asked for drink, drink came.
He asked for ghosts, ghosts came.
He asked for torture, torture came.
He asked for death, death happened.

Now don't go looking for these *kalpavrishkas* in the forest.
You can barely find a tree, these days.

A well established mind, a mind which is in a state of *sambjunkti,*
is referred to as a *Kalpavriksha.*

If you organize your mind,
to a certain level of organization,
it in turn organizes the whole system.
Your body, your emotion, your energies,
everything gets organized in that direction.

Once these *four dimensions of you,*
your physical body, your *mind,* your *emotion,* and the *fundamental life energies*
are *organized* in one *direction,*
once you are like this,
anything that you wish happens,
without even lifting a little finger, actually.

It would help to assist it with activity,
but *even without doing any activity,*
you can still *manifest* what you want,
if you organize these *four dimensions* in one *direction*
and keep it *unwavering* in that *direction* for a *certain period of time.*

Right now the problem with your mind is every moment it is changing its direction.

It is like you want to travel somewhere, and every two steps if you keep changing your direction,
the question of you reaching the destination is very remote.

Unless it happens by *chance*.
So *organizing our minds,*
and in turn *organizing the whole system,*
and these *four basic dimensions* of who you are right now,
in one *direction,*
if you do this,
you are a *Kalpavriksha* yourself.

Anything you wish will happen.

But right now if you look at your lives,
everything you have wished for until now,
if it happens,
you're finished.

Everything and everybody that you have desired for,
if all of that lands up in your house today,
could you live with that?

Once we are empowered like this it is very important that our physical action, emotional action,
mental action, and energy action are controlled and properly directed.

If it is not so, then we become destructive.

Self-Destructive.

Right now, that is our problem.

The technology, which is suppose to make our life beautiful and easy,
has become the source of all the problem,
that we are destroying the very basis of our life,
which is the *Planet.*

So what should have been a boon we are making a curse out of it.

What has brought incredible levels of comfort and convenience to us in the last hundred years or
so has also become a threat to our life simply because we are not in *conscious action,*
we are in a compulsive state of action.

So organizing our minds fundamentally means moving from a compulsive state of activity to a
conscious state of activity.

You might have heard of people, for whom they ask for something and *beyond all expectations* it came true for them.

Generally this happens to people who are in *faith.*

Now let's say you want to build a house.

If you start thinking,
'Oh i want to build a house.
To build a house i need 50 Dollars but i only have 50 cents in my pocket,
not possible, not possible, not possible.'

The moment you say Not Possible, you are also saying I Don't Want It.

So on one level you are creating a desire that you want something,
on another level you are saying i don't want it.
So in this conflict, it may not happen.

'Someone who has some faith in a god or a in a temple or whatever,
Who is simple minded,
faith works only for those people who are simple minded,
thinking people, people who are too much thinking,
for them it never works.

A childlike person who has a simple faith in his god or his temple or whatever,
he goes to the temple and says,
'Shiva, i want a house, i don't know how, you must make it for me.'

Now in his mind there are no negative thoughts.
'Will it happen, will it not happen, is it possible, is it not possible,'
these things are completely removed by this simple Act Of Faith.

Now he believes Shiva will do it for him, and it will happen.

So is Shiva going to come and build your house?

No, i want you to understand, God will not lift his little finger for you.

What you refer to as God, is a Source Of Creation.

As a *creator,* he has done a *phenomenal* job.

There is no question about it.

Could you think of a better Creation than this?

Is it in anybody's imagination to think anything better than what is right now?

So as a Creator, he has done his job wonderfully well.

But if you want life to happen the way you want it,
because right now the very *crux* of your happiness and well-being is this,
if at all you are unhappy,
the only and only reason why you are unhappy is,
life is not happening the way you think it should happen.

That's all it is.

So if life is not happening the way you think it is or should happen,
You are unhappy.

*If life happens the way you think it should happen,
You are happy.*

It's as simple as that.

So if life has to happen the way you think it should happen,
first of all how you *think,*
with how much *focus* you think,
how much *stability* is there in your *thought,*
and how much *reverbarance i*s there in the *thought process,*
will determine whether or not it will become *a reality* or is it just an empty thought,
or how you do not create any impediments for your thought by creating a negative thought
process.

This possible, is something possible or not possible, is destroying humanity.

What is possible and not possible is not your business, it's nature's business.

Your business is just to strive for what you want.

Right now, you are sitting hare, if i ask you two simple questions,
i want you to just look at this and answer this,
right now from where you are sitting,
can you just fly off,
you say *no,*
right now from where you are sitting,
can you get up and walk,
you say *yes,*
what is the basis of this,
why you say no to flying and yes to walking,
is because past experience of life;
many times you have gotten up and walked,
never did you fly off.

Or in other words,
you're using the *past experience of life,*
as a basis,
for *deciding,*
whether something is *possible or not possible.*

Or in other words,
You have *decided,*
What has not happened until now,
Cannot happen in your life in future.

This is a disgrace to humanity,
and the human spirit.

What has not happened until now,
on this planet,

can happen tomorrow.

Human beings are capable of making it happen.

So *what is possible,*
and *what is not possible,*
is *not your business.*

That is nature's business.

Nature will decide that.

You just see what is it that you really want.

And strive for that.

And if your thought is created in a powerful way,
without any negativity,
without any negative thoughts bringing down the intensity of the thought process,
the first and foremost thing is,
you must be clear,
what is it you really want,
if you do not know what you want,
the question of creating it doesn't arise.

If you look at what you really want,
what every human being wants is,

he wants to *live joyfully,*
he wants to *live peacefully,*
in terms of his *relationships* he wants it to be *loving and affectionate,*
or in other words,
all that any human being is seeking is,
pleasantness within himself,
pleasantness around him.

This *pleasantness,*
if it happens in our *body,*
we call this *health* and *pleasure.*

If it happens in our mind,
we call this *peace* and *joy.*

If it happens in our *emotion,*
we call this *love* and *compassion.*

If it happens in our *energy,*
we call this *blissfulness* and *ecstasy.*

This is all that a human being is looking for.

Whether he is going to his office to work,
he wants to make money,
build a carrier,
build a family,
he sits in the bar,
sits in the temple,
he is still looking for the same thing:

Pleasantness within,
Pleasantness around.

If this is what *we want to create,*
i think it's time we *addressed it directly,*

and *commit* ourselves to *creating it.*

So you want to create yourself,
as a,
peaceful human being,
joyful human being,
loving human being,
a pleasant human being on all levels.

And do you also want a world like this?

A peaceful world.

A loving world.

A joyful world.

'No no i want greenery, i want food,'

When we say a joyful world that means everything you want has happened.

So this is all that you are looking for.

So all you need to do is *commit yourself* to *creating it.*

To create a peaceful, joyful, and loving world.

Both for *yourself* and *everybody around you.*

Every day if you start your day with this simple thought in mind,

'That today, wherever i go,
i will create a peaceful, loving,
and joyful world,'

If you fall down one-hundred times in the day,
what does it matter?

For a committed man there is no such thing as failure.

If you fall down a hundred times,
One hundred lessons to be learned.

If you commit yourself like this to creating what you really care for,
Now your mind gets *organized*!

Once your *mind* gets *organized,*
The way you *think* is the way you *feel,*
Your *emotions* get *organized.*

Once your *emotions* get *organized,*
Your *energies* will get *organized,*
in the same *direction.*

Once your thought, emotion, and energies are organized,
your very body will get organized.

Once all these four are *organized* in one *direction,*
Your ability to *create and manifest* what you want is *phenomenal.*

You are the creator in many ways.

That which is the source of creation,
Is functioning within you every moment of your life.

It is just that, have you kept access to that dimension or not?

Organizing the four basic elements of your life,

Will give you that access.

There are *tools and technologies* to do this.

The whole *science of yoga,*
The whole *technology* referred to as *yoga,*
Is just about this,
Transforming yourself from being just a piece of creation,
To become a *creator.*

*"it is my wish and my blessing that
every human being in this world,
should have this access
to the source of creation within himself,
so that he can function here as a creator,
not just as a piece of creation."* -sadhguru

*"for one who knows how to see,
everything is in transition,
for one who knows how to love,
everything is forgivable,"* -krishnamurti

namast'e

namast'e

namast'e

namast'e

namast'e

namast'e

namast'e

namast'e

namast'e

Printed in Great Britain
by Amazon